Christ Died for Your Enemy

Veneta Ford

© Copyright 2019 Veneta Ford

All rights reserved. No part of this collection may be reproduced or transmitted in any form or by any means, electronic or mechanical, including photocopying and recording, or by any information storage and retrieval system, except in the case of brief quotations for use in articles and reviews, without written permission from the author.

710-T Cherry Park Dr, Ste 224
Houston, TX 77095
713-766-4271

ISBN: 9781684118533

Table of Contents

Foreword iv

Chapter 1: Offenses Will Come 1

Chapter 2: Why and How to Pray for Our Enemies? 11

Chapter 3: Coming to Christ Daily 19

Chapter 4: Anger Will Make Us Sick! 27

Chapter 5: The Six Attributes of the Holy Spirit 33

Chapter 6: Released to The Tormentors? 45

Chapter 7: Relationships 51

Chapter 8: Hatred 61

Chapter 9: Navigating A Troubled Marriage 67

Chapter 10: The Ministry of Reconciliation 77

APPENDIX A: How to Be Born Again 87

Foreword

In this book, successful real estate professional and Christian minister Veneta Ford offers clear instruction on dealing with offenses and with one's enemies.

Each of us has been offended at one time or another, and we will certainly be in the days ahead. We've all experienced the pain of betrayal. As is sometimes said, "Judases are provided." Why? To teach us to trust God and love others.

Veneta points out that we were born with a need to trust. But our trust must be in God alone. The old church hymn, "Stand Up, Stand Up for Jesus" has within it an important phrase which says, "The arm of flesh will fail you; you dare not trust your own." The truth is, you dare not place your full trust in anyone but God, who never fails.

However, at one time or another, we all found ourselves shattered by the untrustworthiness of man. Unfortunately, there is little specific instruction for us in how to handle those disappointing and often painful experiences.

In this book, Veneta clearly shows us how to process these disappointments to maintain our mental, emotional, and spiritual health.

She reveals dangers that await those who embrace anger, unforgiveness, and bitterness. For those who struggle with marital problems, there is enlightenment and suggested solutions in Chapter 9: *Navigating A Troubled Marriage*. Marriage is almost a perfect laboratory to prove biblical relationship principles.

Then in Chapter 10, Veneta explains the ministry each of us is to perform. Every believer is to be a minister of reconciliation.

To reconcile means to restore. We cannot expect people to respect our witness for them to be reconciled to God, as long as we are not reconciled with others.

I heartily recommend Veneta's book to you as a resource for personal, or group study.

--**Eddie Smith**, Exec. Director
U.S. Prayer Center in Houston, TX

Chapter 1

Offenses Will Come

Every one of us has been offended at one time or other. Who offended you? Was it a family member, a significant other, a neighbor, a spouse, a child, a classmate, a colleague, a teacher, preacher or parent? One thing is for certain. We tend to feel uncomfortable around those who have offended us or has offended someone we love. We no longer trust anyone who betrays us.

When I was a very young innocent girl, I was staying in the home of a relative one night, when a lot of people came over to their house. I'm not even sure what the celebration was. All I know is that one of them, a young man, took me to a part of the house where we were alone, and in a few minutes, he did terrible sexual things to me that I struggled to block from my mind for years.

Years later, Evangelist Jack Frost, came to preach in our church. After one message, he invited all of those who were victims of sexual abuse to come to the altar for prayer. I didn't go. I didn't want to recall what that boy had done to me that awful night.

Once those seeking help were at the altar, Bro. Frost invited everyone to stand. Then he made a second appeal. "I also want to pray over you who have blocked out things that happened to you as a child." With that, I moved to the front and joined them. I instantly envisioned the details of what had happened to me.

Later I asked my parents if my memory was correct. They assured me that it was. I asked them, "Did you call the police?" They said that they hadn't. I didn't bother to ask them why they hadn't. At that moment, I remember how vulnerable, and unprotected I felt.

Why wouldn't they have reported it to the police? But back then, family things were kept "family." They likely thought they should keep the matter private to protect me. I often thought that had they reported it, they might have prevented him from molesting another child. Those negative thoughts rattled around in my mind for many years.

Around the age of five, I met the Holy Spirit. He drew me to new life in Christ, and I was born again. The depths of that born again experience I would learn later. All I knew was that I was now in Christ and He was in me.

[Author Note: Before we proceed, if you have never had this experience, and do not know that if you died tonight, you'd be in heaven with Him. I encourage you to stop here and carefully read Appendix A in the back of this book.]

Although my salvation experience was instant, my deliverance and understanding of it, were more gradual. It would be awhile before I began to understand the depth of what Christ had done for me and in me. As Scripture says, "And ye shall know the truth, and the truth shall make you free" (John 8:32).

You see, our struggle to come out of darkness into the light isn't a struggle with flesh and blood. It's against spiritual wickedness (evil spirits). The Apostle Paul stated it like this.

"For our struggle is not against flesh and blood, but against the rulers, against the authorities, against the powers of this dark world and against the spiritual forces of evil in the heavenly realms" (Ephesians 6:12).

My husband Bryan and I are real estate investors, and real estate agents. As a business owner, there have been times when I have had to release someone from employment because of their failure to perform. In my role as a realtor, I've even had to let difficult clients go as well. Being a sensitive person, it's always been an emotional ordeal for me to bring them into my office and let them go.

Occasionally, former employees would choose to become my enemy. I would sometimes carry that burden for months, even for years. For self-protection, I would pray that the Lord would bless them quickly with a new job. I didn't want to be hated. I didn't want to deal with the possibility of seeing them again. I just wanted them to move on.

At times, we have had to evict families from their homes due to their failure to pay their mortgages. It was one of the most difficult things for me to do. Once an angry homeowner would argue with me, I would gear up to give them a piece of my mind with a comeback like, "How long have you lived here for free, and not made a single mortgage payment?" Their anger, plus now their embarrassment, would provoke them to "fighting mode." I've even had them pull knives and point guns at me. In my fleshly mind, I wanted to hurt them for hurting me.

I am by no means a large person, so the thought of me fighting them was ridiculous. They could have taken my life easily, simply because I wouldn't shut my big mouth. It has been said, "it does little good to win a battle and lose the war." That was clearly *not* being led by the Holy Spirit. I was behaving as a child, not as a child of God. God began to deal with me more and more as I evicted more families. After all, this was my job as a REO agent.

Early one morning I went to evict a lady who was a known prostitute. That morning, before I left, I spent some time in prayer. Although she wasn't there when I arrived, she returned while we were changing the locks. I greeted her and began to pray with her on the front steps. Two weeks later she called to tell me she had a new job and was no longer prostituting herself. Wow! Go God! Because I had been in prayer earlier that morning, the love of Christ was able to blossom in that situation, and He extended His love through me. He will move in unique ways when we prepare ourselves for Him. I was ready for God to show up in all of my evictions.

I'm certain that, like you, I have enemies. After all, no one can please everyone all the time. But I no longer focus on flesh and blood enemies. I understand that Satan provokes and promotes anger, resentment, and hatred, because he is the enemy of us all.

If we begin each day in God's presence, we will be better prepared for life's challenges, including challenging people. They will always be around, and we will encounter them along the way. Our role is to understand that to deal with them effectively, we'll need to also recognize when we are dealing with the devil. To distinguish between the two will require Spirit-led discernment.

Jesus told us in Matthew 11:28-30 to lean on Him. He said, *"Come to me, all you who are weary and burdened, and I will give you rest. [29] Take my yoke upon you and learn from me, for I am gentle and humble in heart, and you will find rest for your souls. [30] For my yoke is easy and my burden is light."*

We are to come to Him with everything. Dealing with angry people (enemies) will weary us. God encourages us to turn our enemies and ourselves over to Him, and He will give us rest.

One of the rules in boxing is that when the referee separates two fighters from a clinch, each is to take a full step back, to prevent either from "sucker-punching" the other. It's a clean break that gives each boxer a quick refresh. Another rule is that boxers can't spit out their mouthpieces on purpose to stop the action and rest.

To fight is wearying. If we allow him to, Satan will lure us into fighting and rob us of our strength and anointing. It's one of his favorite tactics. Don't fall for it. When we are fighting someone, we are not at rest. Spiritual rest is only found in the presence of the Lord. Being drawn into a bitter matter will drain us mentally, spiritually, emotionally, and physically. When we turn to Him in those times, He puts our souls at rest.

This is an easy principle to learn, but difficult to remember and put into effect when we are suddenly confronted by a challenging person. You see, when we become lazy or distracted, and fail to meet with Him daily, our hearts become hardened and insensitive. Our only solution at that point is to repent and return to fellowship with Him to reestablish His rest.

Early one morning I awoke so mentally tormented about a broken, anger-filled relationship, I was almost sick. I climbed out of bed and went to my quiet place. There, I drew near to Christ, and as He promised, He drew near to me. As I spent time in His presence, He relieved me of the torment. He is the Prince of Peace, who keeps us in perfect peace when our minds are stayed on Him. (Isaiah 9:6; 26:3)

As I sat with my focus on Him, I heard in my spirit, Ephesians 6:11, which says we are to *"put on the full armor of God, so that you can take your stand against the devil's schemes."*

What about you? Are you wearing the full armor of God?

- Do you have the helmet of salvation on your head? Do you know without a doubt that you are born again?
- Is the belt of truth around your waist? Are you growing in your knowledge of Scripture, God's truth?
- Do you exhibit His righteousness, which is the breastplate of righteousness?
- Are you wearing your gospel shoes? Do you share

Christ with others?

- Do you carry the sword of the Spirit?

The Eleventh Commandment

Virtually all of us are at least familiar with the 10 Commandments that God gave to Moses on the mountain in Exodus 20. However, many don't know about the 11th Commandment, the one Jesus gave us in John 13:34, when He said, *"A new command I give you: Love one another. As I have loved you, so you must love one another. 34 By this everyone will know that you are my disciples, if you love one another."*

Thomas à Kempis, the medieval German-Dutch author of *The Imitation of Christ*, which is one of the most popular and best-known Christian books on devotion said, "In Jesus and for Him, enemies and friends alike are to be loved."

If we are serious about following Christ, being Holy Spirit-led believers, we will put on the full armor of God each day, humble ourselves, and allow His love to rule in our hearts.

Please pray this with me: "Whatever it takes Lord, soften my heart to be dependent on you; to forgive and repent quickly; and to love others as you love me. Forgive me for doing things on my own, and for the times I've engaged angry people in the power of my flesh, rather than Your Spirit. Forgive me for being easily distracted, and for failing to keep my focus on you. Here is my heart, Lord. Fill me with Your peace. Lord, I choose to follow you. In Jesus' Name I pray, amen."

> "… those who belong to Christ Jesus have crucified the flesh with its passions and desires"
> Galatians 5:24).

Forgiveness isn't about keeping score.

It's about *losing count.*

Chapter 2

Why and How to Pray for Our Enemies?

I don't know about you, but I admit, there have been times when I wanted to pray *the worst* for my enemies. I wanted to see them judged. But look what Jesus said in His Sermon on The Mount:

"You have heard that it was said, 'Love your neighbor and hate your enemy. [44] *But I tell you, love your enemies and pray for those who persecute you,* [45] *that you may be children of your Father in heaven"* (Matthew 5:43).

Jesus' radical teaching like this made it difficult for people to commit to follow Him when He walked the earth. It was hardest for the elite "religious professionals."

Are you familiar with the term, "frenemy?" A frenemy is one who pretends to be a friend but is really an enemy. Do we pretend to be friends with some, perhaps coworkers, while we talk badly about them behind their backs? Instead, let's begin to put them on our prayer lists, and pray for God to bless them. The late civil rights activist, Martin Luther King, Jr. once said, "In the end, we will remember not the words of our enemies, but the silence of our friends." Let's let our voices be heard on behalf of our friends and our enemies especially in prayer.

Since the day God chose Abraham, through whom He would establish a new nation, Israel's Jewish people have been mistreated, hated and even enslaved. Their enemies have abounded from Egypt, to the Roman Empire, to Nazi Germany. Today, hateful Islamic groups like Iran and ISIS seek Israel's annihilation. For Jesus to tell the Jews of His day to pray for their enemies was like telling the Jews today to pray for their sworn enemies, Hamas, Iran or ISIS.

Jesus went as far as to say that to pray for our enemies would prove to the world that we are children of the Father. Some Christians, upon hearing this, conclude that Jesus only meant for us to pray for our enemies to be born again. That would bless them of course, but that isn't what He had in mind. His instruction well went beyond that.

In the next verse, Matthew 5:44, Jesus continues, *"...Love your enemies."* Love doesn't mean that we are to simply "tolerate them." Love is an action word, a verb. Love is what we do, not what we feel. To that, He adds, *"Bless them that curse you."* Then, *"Do good to them who despitefully use you and persecute you."*

The Apostle Paul picked up this most unusual theme in Romans 12:17-18, saying, *"Do not repay anyone evil for evil...if it is possible, as far as it depends on you, live at peace with everyone."* In verse 19 Paul warns, *"Do not take revenge."* Then he concludes in verses 20-21 as He quotes Proverbs 25:21-22 saying, *"On the contrary: 'If your enemy is hungry, feed him; if he is thirsty, give him something to drink. In doing this, you will heap burning coals on his head.' Do not be overcome by evil, but overcome evil with good."*

How could "heaping burning coals on someone's head" be a blessing? I only recall one place in Scripture where something like that appears. It was on the Day of Pentecost, when the Holy Spirit was poured out, that "tongues of fire" appeared on people's heads. Coals of fire, embers, might be thought of as "pre-fire." Perhaps this passage suggests that our acts of kindness to our enemies will prepare the way for the Holy Spirit to touch them. You may recall that in Luke 15:2 Jesus was accused of being *"a friend of sinners."* Certainly, He was. After all, He died to rescue sinners from eternal separation from the Father. He was accused of being *"a glutton, and a drunkard, a friend of tax collectors and sinners"* (Luke 7:34). Tax collectors were hated in His day. Although He was no glutton or drunkard, Jesus was a friend of tax collectors and sinners. In fact, He loved them *"in that while we were still sinners, Christ died for us"* (Romans 5:8) It was more than a feeling. It was what He did for them. He died for, and in the place of sinners. That's love!

To pray for our enemies, those who've sinned against us, may change them. However, it will surely change us; and without the help of the Holy Spirit, none of this is possible? It isn't easy for us to pray for God to bless people who have hurt us and perhaps, tried to destroy us. But remember that Matthew 5:43 ". . . *so that you may be sons* (prove that you are sons) *of your Father who is in heaven."* It's a testimony that we truly are sons of the Father—that we've been born again. Wow!

It reminds me of the phrase, "Like father, like son." Our Father loves sinners, yet He hates sin. Why? Because He created sinners in His image, to reflect His likeness. Their sin has marred it. As was true of us, sin is killing them and will prevent them from reaching their kingdom potential. (Romans 3:23; 6:23) He sent Christ to rescue them from the kingdom of darkness and translocate them in His kingdom of light. Since He loves them that much, He is right to expect us to pray for His best in their lives. As the late Evangelist Billy Graham has said, "It's the Holy Spirit's job to convict. God's job to judge, and my job to love."

When we pray for our enemies, we enter into partnership with the Father, on their behalf. We can't stop people from being our enemies, but we can stop ourselves from being theirs. And as we align ourselves with Him, He will flow through us in other areas of life too. As we pray for their salvation, their lives, health, families, and businesses, we should also pray for them to be restrained from evil doing. We must pray for the evil they do to be restrained. Jesus, in His model prayer, taught us to pray for ourselves not to be led into temptation, but to be delivered from evil. (Matthew 6:9-13)

It's important that we not rejoice in their suffering. In Proverbs 24:17 we are instructed, *"Do not gloat when your enemy falls; when they stumble, do not let* your heart *rejoice."* Notice, we are not to allow *our hearts* to rejoice. Sometimes, we behave on the outside, while we're misbehaving on the inside. Never forget, some of the greatest Christians of all time, were the greatest sinners before they met Him! The Apostle Paul, and John Newton the former slave trader who after he found Christ, composed the familiar hymn, "Amazing Grace," immediately came to mind. We may someday find out that Paul's salvation was the result of someone he persecuted praying for him; and that John Newton's transformation was a result of the prayers of one of the slaves of whom he took advantage. Paul warned us not to allow evil to overcome us. What does that mean? It means that we are to guard our hearts lest the evil done to us cause us to react with evil. James 2:13 says that "*. . . judgment without mercy will be shown to anyone who has not been merciful. <u>Mercy triumphs over judgment</u>.*"

Don't allow anyone to make you their enemy. Why would you allow another person to control you—to make you do anything.

Wake up each morning with a heart desire to bless others. Don't allow your pressing activities to deter you from remaining meaningfully connected with Christ. Your mission is more important than your business, your titles, or your net worth.

Lamentations 3:22-23 tells us, *"Because of the LORD's great love we are not consumed, for his compassions never fail. They are new every morning; great is your* (His) *faithfulness."* Our agenda is the Lord Jesus, and to bring others to Him. Each day is a new day in Him, with new mercies. That means, a NEW me and a new you!

The next time someone cuts you off in traffic, begin to pray a blessing over them. Do it out of obedience to Him; and in time, you'll experience such a heart-change that it will become the desire of your heart—second nature. Owen Feltham has said, "It is much safer to reconcile an enemy than to conquer him; victory may deprive him of his poison, but reconciliation of his will."

Please pray this with me: "Lord, Master of all enemies and friends, help me to love as You love. Holy Spirit remind me to call upon you when I deal with difficult people. Remind me to call on you to empower me to restrain my anger and not be vengeful. Jesus, love others through me. Allow me to see them as You see them. Change my heart, O God. I submit myself to you. In Jesus' Name I pray, amen."

"Three things last forever--faith, hope, and love--and the greatest of these is love" (1 Corinthians 13:13).

"My Command is this: Love each other as I have loved you" (John 15:12).

"Above all, love each other deeply, because love covers over a multitude of sins" (1 Peter 4:8).

Why do we feel the need to demand justice?
It's because God created us in His image, and He demands it.
However, like God, we must accept the fact that Christ has met the requirements of justice.

To *pray for* those we don't like, is ultimate grace.

Chapter 3

Coming to Christ Daily

We Americans value our independence. After all, we fought a war to gain it. Then we signed a "Declaration of Independence" in 1776, which we highly value to this day.

Independence can be a good thing, in the right application. However, independence, wrongly applied can ruin things.

Take marriage for example. Some marriages suffer because one or both partners entered the relationship *before* they gained their independence. Either the husband or wife is still dependent upon their parents. Every time they have a dispute, one or the other runs to their mother or father for emotional, even financial support. Scripture clearly teaches, *"That is why a man leaves his father and mother and is united to his wife, and they become one flesh"* (Genesis 2:24). This is such a strategic verse, Matthew and Mark quote it, as does the Apostle Paul in his letter to the Christians in Ephesus. (Matthew 19:5; Mark 10:7; and Ephesians 5:31).

You see, marriage was never meant for two independent people. A biblical marriage is composed of a co-dependency where a husband and wife become one, mutually dependent on each other and the Lord. However, until a person is independent, they have nothing to offer.

The healthiest marriages are a result of a man and woman who have left father and mother, each has become independent, and they willingly give themselves to the other. It couldn't be stated more clearly than 1 Corinthians 7:3-5. *"The husband should fulfill his marital duty to his wife, and likewise the wife to her husband. The wife does not have authority over her own body, but the husband. Likewise, the husband does not have authority over his own body, but the wife."*

Adam and Eve, in the Garden of Eden, were dependent upon God until deceived by the serpent (Satan). They yielded to sin and became independent of God, and as a result, He evicted them from their paradise.

When we discover that we are sinners, and that our sin has (as Adam and Eve's did) separated us from God, we can repent and declare our dependency upon Him. By inviting Him into our hearts to be our *Lord*, on whom we can lean for direction; and our *Savior*, upon whom we can depend for life, we are born again. From that day forward, as the husband and wife are one (in the illustration above), we are one with Christ. In a spiritual sense, we are His bride and He is our Bridegroom. Paul stated it this way. *"But whoever is united with the Lord is one with him in spirit"* (1 Corinthians 6:17).

So, from the day we are born again, we are to totally depend upon Christ Jesus. The true Christian life is Christ, living in us. You can't live my life, the Veneta life; nor can I live yours. Likewise, neither of us can live the Christian life-- Christ's life. Only our resurrected Christ can do that. He does that in and through us. In Galatians 2:20 Paul expressed his dependency upon Christ, saying, *"I have been crucified with*

Christ and I no longer live, but Christ lives in me. *The life I now live in the body, I live by faith in the Son of God, who loved me and gave himself for me."*

Day-by-day, hour-by-hour, moment-by-moment we are to be submitted to Christ's lordship as He lives His life through us.

Peace with God

How do we make peace with our enemies? It begins by finding peace within our own hearts. When we are born again, we are given *"peace with God."* (Romans 5:1) Our sin that separated us from Him is *gone*, not covered, as was the case in the Old Testament. *Sin in those days was covered*, because it was yet to be paid for. Each animal that was sacrificed for sin, in the Old Testament, was like the swipe of a credit card. Sin was considered forgiven, yet to be paid for. The sin was covered, like the use of *White-Out®*, the correction fluid covers typing errors.

However, the moment the Lamb of God (Jesus) sacrificed His life for the sins of the world, the sin accounts of the faithful Old Testament believers were justified. Their sin accounts were closed. Today, when we accept Him and His sacrifice for our sin, *our sins are eradicated*, never to be mentioned against us again. *"If we confess our sins, he is faithful and just and will forgive us our sins and purify us from all unrighteousness"* (1 John 1:9). He promises us in Hebrews 8:12, *". . . I will forgive their wickedness and will remember their sins no more."*

The peace of God

Not only did we find *peace <u>with</u> God* when we were born again, we are also given the *peace <u>of</u> God*. Jesus said, *"Peace I leave with you; <u>my peace I give you</u>. I do not give to you as the world gives. Do not let your hearts be troubled and do not be afraid"* (John 14:27).

Perfect peace

Finally, we are offered *perfect peace!* Isaiah 26:3 says, *"You keep him in <u>perfect peace</u> whose mind is stayed on you, because he trusts in you."*

An aside: Has it ever occurred to you that the greatest sinner of all time was Jesus, God's sinless Son—by imputation? God imputed (placed on Jesus) the sins of the entire world. As the old hymn says, *"Jesus paid it all. All to Him I owe. Sin had left a crimson stain. He washed it white as snow."* PTL!

So, with Christ in our hearts, by His Spirit, we are to submit to His leadership in all things. Remember, we are to be "crucified with Christ." Dead people make no decisions. We are to continually depend on Him. This is especially true in our relationships.

I have a pastor friend who confesses that he and his mother had difficulty maintaining a harmonious relationship, once he was grown. When he and his wife would go to visit his parents, after dinner, and sometimes at the dinner table, he and his mother would get into a discussion that would escalate to an uncomfortable level. They loved each other, but they shared similar personality traits, so their differences of opinions would typically ruin the family fellowship. It was so bad that rather than stay at his parent's house, they would stay at a nearby hotel. That way, when dinner was over, they could leave and escape any uncomfortable conversations.

My friend said that after several years, the Lord convicted him of his behavior and told him that he was to give God ownership of all his possessions, and allow God to fill all of his positions. His positions included husband, father, employee, employer, brother, uncle, and more. And of course, one was his position as his mother's son. God said, "You have made a mess of things. Why not allow me to take that position for you."

The next time his mother called, he said, "Lord, here she is. Would you please take this call?"

She said, "Hello, son. How are you and the family? And after some "small talk," she would make a statement that have normally provoked him. Always before, he would say, "Mother, I totally disagree, for the following three reasons..." This time however, the Father's perfect peace rested on him and he said, "Mother, that's certainly one way to look at it." The Holy Spirit gave him grace to avoid any conflict.

When the conversation ended, he said, "Mother, I love you." She responded, "Love you too."

Month-by-month, when she would call, he would turn the call over to Jesus. As he did, she began to change. She became calmer, less argumentative, and would end their conversations with, "Well, I just wanted to call and check on you, Son. I love you so much and miss seeing you."

His last few years with her before she passed, they would always stay in his parent's home. And they would have deep discussions, complete with peaceful, loving, submissive disagreements at times, but never an argument or the slightest tension.

Christ, the Prince of Peace, is to be our life. So, if we are not peaceful, it's a sure sign that He isn't Lord of our lives. It's this mindset that helps calm and mend bitter relationships. We can and should always be quick to forgive others as He has forgiven us. However, reconciliation with those who choose to be our enemies won't always be possible. In those cases, we can still show forth Christ's love as a testimony to them.

It's an exciting life, living totally dependent upon the Lord, and watching Him touch lives of those around us. It's the atmosphere for miracles.

Please pray this with me: "Whatever it takes Lord, soften my heart to be dependent on you; to forgive and repent quickly; and to love others as you love me. Forgive me for doing things on my own, and for the times I've engaged angry people in the power of my flesh, rather than Your Spirit. Forgive me for being easily distracted, and for failing to keep my focus on you. Here is my heart, Lord. Fill me with Your peace. Lord, I choose to follow you. In Jesus' Name I pray, amen."

Chapter 4

Anger Will Make Us Sick!

The results of many studies have shown the unhealthy results unresolved anger. Here are a few:

- Headaches
- Digestive imbalances
- Insomnia
- Anxiety
- Depression
- High Blood Pressure
- Skin Problems, including eczema
- Heart Attack

- Stroke

Heart health

According to Jenny Hope, Medical Correspondent for the Daily Mail, "Losing your temper can trigger a heart attack – even as long as two hours after the anger has subsided, researchers have warned."

Dr. Chris Aiken, an instructor in clinical psychiatry at the Wake Forest University School of Medicine and director of the Mood Treatment Center in Winston-Salem, North Carolina wrote, "In the two hours after an angry outburst, the chance of having a heart attack doubles." A research project released in 2009 showed that an angry heart can lead to sudden death. Before flying hot, the next time someone irritates you, ask the Holy Spirit to help you control yourself. These sudden deaths are somewhere around 400,000 a year.

Brain health

What does anger do to our brains? The adrenal glands flood the body with stress hormones, such as adrenaline and cortisol. The brain shunts blood away from the gut and toward the muscles, in preparation for physical exertion. One study found that there were three times higher risk of having a stroke from a blood clot to the brain or bleeding within the brain during the two-hours after an angry outburst.

Circulatory health

The exact cause of type 2 Diabetes still is unclear. However, recent studies suggest that not only depression, but also general emotional stress and anxiety, sleeping problems, anger and hostility are associated with an increased risk for the development of type 2 Diabetes.

Immune health

Anger weakens your immune system. In one study, Harvard University scientists found that in healthy people, simply recalling and angry experience from their past caused a six-hour dip in levels of the antibody immunoglobulin A, the cell's first line of defense against infection.

Mental health

Anger makes anxiety worse. If you are a worrier, it's important to know that anxiety and anger can go together. You'll recall Paul's instruction to the Christians in Philippi to be anxious for nothing, but to pray with thanksgiving.

He went on to promise that by doing so, God will keep our hearts and minds at peace. (Philippians 4:6-7) Anxiety (worry) is the sin of calling into question the trustworthiness of our God. And anger is linked to depression.

Respiratory health

Hostility can hurt your lungs. Even if you are not a smoker, you can still be hurting your lungs if you're a perpetually angry, hostile person.

A group of Harvard University scientists studied 670 men over eight years using a hostility scale scoring method to measure anger levels and assessed any changes in the men's lung function. The men with the highest hostility ratings had significantly worse lung capacity, which increased their risk of respiratory problems. Researchers theorized that an uptick in stress hormones, which are associated with feelings of anger, creates inflammation in the airways.

General health

Anger can shorten your life. "Stress is very tightly linked to general health. If you're stressed and angry, you'll shorten your lifespan," says Mary Fristad, PhD, a professor of psychiatry and psychology at the Ohio State University. A 17-year *University of Michigan* study found that couples who hold in their anger have a shorter life span than those who readily say when they're mad.

Let's each spend time with the Lord and ask Him if we have any unresolved issues, anger, or unforgiveness in our hearts of which we are unaware. Unaware? Really? Yes. None of us can keep track of all our faults. You may recall Psalm 19:12, where the Psalmist prayed, *"Who can discern their own errors? Forgive my hidden faults."*

The sad fact is that there are many today who are saved, but not yet free. The precious Master will show us what we need to be cleansed of so we can move to the next level. God wants us totally free in Christ. John wrote, *". . . if the Son sets you free, you will be free indeed"* (John 8:36).

Once the Lord reveals any secret sins of unforgiveness, and we confess and receive His cleansing, we can live our best life. We will be able to hear Him more clearly. We will notice His miracles in our lives. To confess is to be cleansed. To confess is to heal. Until we confess, we cannot heal.

Please pray this with me: *"Lord, my body is your home-- your temple. I submit it to you as a living sacrifice, holy and acceptable to You. I commit today to feed it and care for it as such. I reject anger and anxiety. I refuse to call into question Your integrity.*

You are my faithful Father--"A good, good Father." Fill me with Your Spirit and flow through me. In Jesus' Name I pray, amen."

"Many are the afflictions of the righteous, but the Lord delivers them all" (Psalm 19:34).

"Do everything in love" (1 Corinthians 16:14).

"Let the morning bring me word of your unfailing love, for I have put my trust in you. Show me the way I should go, for to you I entrust my life" (Psalm 143:8).

"And over all these virtues put on love, which binds them all together in perfect unity" (Colossians 3:14).

"And so we know and rely on the love God has for us. God is love. Whoever lives in love lives in God, and God in them" (1 John 4:16).

If you are emotionally sick, you'll find offense in virtually anything and with anyone. However, an emotionally healthy person understands that others' actions are a result of unhealed hurt. They see the opportunity to love like Christ. Joseph was a great example.

Chapter 5

The Six Attributes of the Holy Spirit

*"The Spirit of the L<small>ORD</small> will rest on him—
the Spirit of <u>wisdom and of understanding</u>,
the Spirit of <u>counsel and of might</u>,
the Spirit of <u>the knowledge and fear of the L<small>ORD</small></u>—
³and he will delight in the fear of the L<small>ORD</small>.
He will not judge by what he sees with his eyes,
or decide by what he hears with his ears"* (Isaiah 11:2-3).

This passage is often referred to as "The Seven Spirits of God." Those who do so, suggest that God's seven spirit are:

1. The Spirit of the Lord.
2. The Spirit of wisdom.

3. The Spirit of understanding.
4. The Spirit of counsel.
5. The Spirit of might.
6. The Spirit of the knowledge.
7. The Spirit of the fear of the Lord.

However, it's important to understand that God *does not* actually have seven spirits. (1 Corinthians 12:13; Ephesians 4:4) As Jesus told the woman at the well, in John 4:24, *"God is A Spirit; and they that worship Him must worship Him in spirit and in truth."* Each of the six attributes mentioned in verse two are attributes of God's *one* Holy Spirit.

Let's look at it more closely.

In verse two, 600-years before Christ was born, Isaiah writes, "THE *Spirit of the LORD will rest on him—.*" It doesn't say, "THESE *Spirits. . ."* Again, the Lord has one Spirit, His Holy Spirit, which this messianic prophecy says will rest upon Israel's Messiah—Jesus Christ. And it certainly did.

Then Isaiah describes three pairs of unique qualities of the Holy Spirit.

He would have the Spirit of Wisdom and Understanding—Evidence of Jesus' wisdom and understanding could be seen as early as 12-years of age, when He was found in the temple in Jerusalem teaching the Scribes and Pharisees. (Luke 2:41-52)

He would have the Spirit of Counsel and Might— *"Wonderful Counselor, Mighty God. . ."* (Isaiah 9:6) No better counsel has been given to man than the Sermon on the Mount recorded in Matthew 5-7. What greater demonstration of might could be found than when having been awakened from a deep sleep in the midst of a storm at sea, Jesus rebuked the wind, and said to the sea, "Peace! Be still!"

He would have the Spirit of Knowledge and the Fear of the Lord— We see this clearly in Jesus' earthly ministry, time after time. One of the clearest was when the scribes accused Him of blasphemy. Matthew writes, *"But Jesus knew what they were thinking and said, 'Why do you harbor evil in your hearts?'"* (Matthew 9:4)

And Jesus' "fear of the Lord," His respect for, and total dependence upon the Father, were renown.

Jesus lived a Spirit-dependent life, as Isaiah prophesied. The Apostle Paul would later write to the Christians in

Philippi, "(Jesus) *Who, being in very nature God, did not consider equality with God something to be used to his own advantage: rather, he made himself nothing by taking the very nature of a servant, being made in human likeness. ⁸ And being found in appearance as a man, he humbled himself by becoming obedient to death—even death on a cross"* (Philippians 2:6-8)!

The Word became flesh.

The incarnation of Christ is one of the most remarkable aspects of Christ's life. When He walked the earth, He was 100% God and 100% man. He was sent to live and to die as a man, for the sins of mankind. We are told that He was tempted in every manner as we are. (Hebrews 4:15)

Consider this:

1. Jesus left His **omnipresence** when He came in human flesh. When He was in Jerusalem, He was not in Nazareth. He was no longer all places at all times.
2. He laid aside His **omnipotence**. He said, "*. . . the Son can do* nothing *by himself; he can only do what he sees his Father doing. . .*" "*By myself I can do nothing, , ,*" (John 5:19; 5:30a, NIV).

3. He laid aside His **omniscience** to live as a man. He didn't know all things while He was here. Some incorrectly suggest that He did, because He told the Samaritan woman He found at the well, that she had been married five times and the man she was living with was not her husband. He couldn't have possibly known that. Being Spirit-indwelt, those facts were revealed to Him by the Holy Spirit. We refer to them as "words of knowledge."

In Matthew 24:36, NIV speaking of when He would come again, Jesus said, *"But about that day or hour no one knows, not even the angels in heaven, <u>nor the Son</u> (Himself), but only the Father."* He admitted that He didn't know.

However, in Acts 1:7a, after His resurrection, prior to His ascension, the disciples asked Him again. His answer was different. He said, *"It's not for you to know. . . "*

It is in that first chapter of Acts that He promises to send His Spirit. He tells them not to leave Jerusalem without the Holy Spirit. (Acts 1:4b)

They would, as we do, need the Holy Spirit to successfully navigate through life and reach their kingdom potential. We especially need the Holy Spirit to resolve issues with our enemies.

In reconciling a broken relationship or betrayal, wisdom and understanding are critical. The Holy Spirit provides those. Counsel and might are requirements, as are knowledge and a proper respect for the Lord. As we walk in the Spirit, these attributes become more and more evident in our lives.

As Jesus prayed for us in John 17:16, He told the Father, *"They (us) are not of the world, even as I am not of it."* I prefer the New Living Translation, which says, *"They do not belong to this world any more than I do."* Isn't that a remarkable thought? Allow that to sink in. We are one with Christ—one with the Creator of the universe! Noted teacher, Lance Wallnau, says, "You must start by ruling your own mind and then. . . you can conquer the mountain."

When we are at odds with someone or they with us, it's easy for our flesh nature (our lower, Adamic nature) to operate, which only exacerbates the matter.

Anger arises, tempers flare, stress hormones secrete, words are said, and sometimes actions taken that fan the flames of division and hatred. The enemy loves to provoke that. It also grieves the Holy Spirit who indwells every true, born again believer.

The Holy Spirit's nature and our flesh nature are opposed one to the other. In a sense, they war against each other. So, when we submit to one, we offend the other, which is why for us to allow our flesh to take control grieves the Holy Spirit. Grief is an interesting word. It's a "love word." We can only grieve someone who loves us. So, to reconcile broken relationships will require the ministry of the Holy Spirit within.

The Ministry of Reconciliation

Paul wrote to the Christians in Corinth, " *if anyone is in Christ, the new creation has come:[a] The old has gone, the new is here! 18 All this is from God, who reconciled us to himself through Christ and gave us the ministry of reconciliation*" (1 Corinthians 5:17-18, NIV) God is a reconciler. He has reconciled us to Himself through Christ. Now, He commissions us to reconcile others to Him. But to do so, we must also be reconciled one to the other.

How did Christ enable us to be reconciled to the Father? He did so by dying in our place. In so doing, He cancelled our sin-debt. God can't relate positively to people in sin. But because of Calvary, we have been made the righteousness of

Christ. God has torn up the charges against us, accepted Christ's payment in our place, and has declared us righteous. He further says that He will never remember our sins against us again. Christ took the judgment for them all. *Jesus paid it all, all to Him we owe, sin had left a crimson stain, He washed it white as snow.* PTL!

Let's read on. *"God was reconciling the world to himself in Christ, not counting people's sins against them. And he has committed to us the message of reconciliation"* (1 Corinthians 5:19).

Our message of reconciliation is this. . .

1. I was separated from God by my sin.
2. I repented for my sin and received His forgiveness.
3. He forgave me, and no longer counts my sin against me.
4. Jesus, who paid for my sin, united me with God, and came to live in my heart.
5. Because He died for you, if you repent of your sin and accept Him and His payment on your behalf, you too can be reconciled with God.

Paul summarizes saying, *"We are therefore Christ's ambassadors, as though God were making his appeal through us. We implore you on Christ's behalf: Be reconciled to God.* [21] *God made him who had no sin to be sin for us, so that in him we might become the righteousness of God"* (1 Corinthians 5:20-21).

What does it mean for us to be "Christ's ambassadors?" An ambassador is one who stands in for another. For example, a U.S. ambassador in a foreign country represents the U.S. and our President. He makes no decisions Himself. He simply says what he is told to say and does what he is told to do. In that regard, we are to be as Christ in this world.

You recall that Jesus only did what He saw the Father doing. (John 5:19) He says, *"As the Father hath sent me, I am sending you"* (John 20:21). John writes further, in 1 John 4:17, *". . . as He is, so are we in this world."* That is a serious calling on each of us.

In 1 John 2:2 John reminds us that, *"He (Christ) is the atoning sacrifice for our sins, and not only for ours but also for the sins of the whole world."* This raises the question, "were we saved by grace alone? Or was it a matter of justice?" The answer is. . . it was both! We were saved by grace (Ephesians 2:8-9). But it was also an act of justice. It was just for God to reconcile us to Himself because Jesus was our sin-sacrifice.

For that reason, we can be reconciled to those who sin against us. We do believe that Christ died for the sins of the whole world, which includes any sin ever committed against us. We accept that His payment for sin at Calvary was enough. Therefore, we refuse to hold hostage those who've sinned against us, awaiting their payment. He paid what they owed us.

We are often encouraged to "forgive and forget." We don't have the capacity to forget at will, as God does. However, we do have the ability to refuse to harbor resentment. We do have the ability to refuse to wish ill upon our enemies. To forgive someone who has offended us, especially one who's deeply offended us, isn't to diminish at all what they have done. Their sin, like ours, was serious. It cost God the life of His Son, Jesus. To diminish it would be dishonest. Sometimes it's not a single large offense, but a series of small offenses. Offenses happen. They can range from one's spouse forgetting their birthday or anniversary; to their being involved in an affair.

God loves sinners. We are also to love sinners, including those who sin against us. Love covers a multitude of sins. (1

Peter 4:8) And we learn in "the love chapter," 1 Corinthians 13, that *"love is patient, love is kind, . . . love does not dishonor others, . . . It is not easily angered; it keeps no record of wrongs* (vss 4-5)! You see, as God forgives us and keeps no record of our wrongs (sins), according to Hebrews 8:12; we are to forgive others and tear up their sin-lists. His grace, mercy and justice converge in our hearts and we release them, without further demands.

Wow! How can that be done? It can only be done as we are indwelt by (filled with) the Holy Spirit, and *"walk in the Spirit."* By walking in the Spirit, *"we will not gratify the desires of the flesh"* (Galatians 5:16).

There is a lot said about being "Spirit-filled." In fact, when it's all said and done, there is a lot more said than done, and entirely too little said about what it truly means. How is this definition? You know you are Spirit-filled, when you are more like Jesus than you are like yourself!

"Therefore, as you have received Christ Jesus the Lord, so walk in Him, having been firmly rooted and now being built up in Him an established in your faith, just as you were instructed, and overflowing with gratitude" (Colossians 2:6-7).

Please pray this with me: "Father, when I was lost in my sin without any interest in You, You loved me. Jesus, you gave Your life for me. You died in my place. I release anyone who has sinned against me. Jesus, you paid the price for the sin of the world. Therefore, based on your payment, I release those who've offended me. Make me an effective minister of reconciliation, so others can find you. In Jesus' Name I pray, amen."

Chapter 6

Released to The Tormentors?

Sally sought counseling for her nicotine addiction. She had taken up smoking as a teen. Now in her early thirties she had become a two-pack-a-day chain smoker.

She was certainly aware of the dangers of smoking, of course. After all, her father, and several of her friends had died of lung cancer, directly related to smoking.

Now, she was ready to quit. But how? She'd tried before and nothing seemed to work. She'd quit for a day or two; and once for two weeks, but always returned to her habit. It seemed that there was no lasting solution.

Born again? She had an experience with Christ as a child and felt certain that He was in her life. In fact, that just added to her shame, guilt, and embarrassment.

What was she to do? Pray? She had prayed. She had begged God for a solution, but no matter how hard she tried, nothing seemed to work.

She seemed driven to smoke, addicted to nicotine, yet every time she lighted a cigarette she felt defeated.

It had been recommended that she see a counselor. That's why she walked into his office that day. She was handed a form to complete, sat down and began filling it out. She even felt ashamed filling out the form.

When she was called in, Dr. Johnson, the counselor, greeted her warmly and invited her to be seated. She had never met him, but he seemed nice enough.

He asked about her and she told him about herself and her family. He looked briefly through the forms she had handed him, turned them over and pushed them aside, then said calmly, "Sally, let's pray."

It wasn't a long prayer, nor did it seem to be a particularly powerful prayer. His prayer was directed at receiving God's guidance.

She was in favor of that. She had sought God's help for more than five years.

With that, Dr. Johnson paused for a moment as if he was listening. Then he said, "Sally, why do you hate your daddy?"

What!? What's that about, she wondered. She was shocked. She replied, "I don't hate my father."

"You didn't like him, right?" the counselor said.

"No Sir, I didn't. Not after the way he treated my mother and our family."

"Sally, you hated him, didn't you?" Dr. Johnson pressed.

"Yes, I did. I hated him!" Sally blurted out angrily, breaking into tears.

"And you still do," Dr. Johnson concluded. You're going to have to release your father if you want to be free. Are you willing to do that?"

Sally nodded, "Yes."

Then Dr. Johnson led her in a prayer of repentance, with a declaration that she was releasing her deceased father."

With that, a heavy weight was lifted from her heart. She felt reborn *again*!

The next day, at noon, she suddenly realized that she hadn't had any desire for a cigarette. In fact, her compulsion to light one up was gone. After two days, she was so liberated from her habit that she discarded her cigarettes, her "back-up" stash in her dresser drawer, her ashtrays, lighters (even the sterling silver one, which had been a gift from her husband.)

She wanted *nothing to do with smoking.*

She called in a carpet cleaning company to steam clean her carpets and drapes. At last, she was a "former smoker." Her heart was a peace. Scripture teaches us to rid ourselves of hatred. (Ephesians 4:31) Hatred causes conflict in our lives. (Proverbs 10:12) She could certainly bear witness to that.

John writes in 1st John 4:20 that if we say we love God, and hate someone, we are liars. This brings to mind the verse where Jesus said that what we've done to others, we've done to Him.

One's hate-filled heart will spiritually blinds them. Why? Because it offends the heavenly Father, who is the Source of enlightenment. He is repelled by it. Thus, to embrace hatred is to become spiritually blind. (1 John 2:9-11)

Perhaps the most serious thing about hate is that God considers it the equivalent of *murder*. John wrote, *"Anyone who hates is brother is a murderer . . ."* (1 John 3:15a)

Please pray this with me: "Soften my heart, Lord. Teach me to never allow hatred to take root in my heart against anyone, regardless of what they might do to me. As you loved me, before I loved you, Lord; teach me to love You and to esteem others better than myself. I choose to follow you. In Jesus' Name I pray, amen."

Chapter 7

Relationships

How important can relationships be? Think about it. Everything, all that is, began with a relationship! Creator God is an eternal tripart being. Though one Person, He is Father, Son and Holy Ghost, the "Three-in-one." Our magnificent Creator exists as a relationship of three Himself!

Throughout history people have sought to understand and explain it. One explanation, commonly heard, is the "egg example." Many share it with children. They show the children an egg. Then asks how many do you see? They answer, of course, one egg.

Then they break the shell and separate the white from the yoke. "Now how many do you see?" They ask. They answer, "three." Correct. There is the shell, the yoke and the white. Each is separate, but all are egg.

With adults, some point out that when Jesus hung on the cross as our sacrificial Savior, He spoke to the Father (a second person). And said to Him, *"Into Thy hands I commend my Spirit."*

Surely you can see that on a child's level, that may make sense. But we don't actually understand our triune God. Nor do we need to prove that He, being One God, exists as three—Father, Son and Holy Spirit. We accept that by faith.

What does "eternal" mean? Eternal means having neither a beginning nor end. God is the only eternal being.

Most of us are familiar with John 3:16. It's the first Bible verse most of us learned. The King James Version reads, *"For God so loved the world, that he gave his only begotten Son, that whosoever believeth in him should not perish, but have* everlasting life.*"* Notice that the result of our believing in Him is that we gain *everlasting life.*

"Everlasting life" is a *quantity*—a length of life. It means to live forever, without end.

But wait. Everyone, whether they know Christ or not, will exist forever. Those of us who are in Christ will be forever with Him. Those who reject Him will suffer everlasting separation from Him. So, *"everlasting life"* is a less than accurate translation. That's why some versions, based on a better understanding of the original Greek, read: *". . . should not perish, but have ETERNAL life."* Eternal life is not a *quantity* of life. It's a *quality* of life! When we trust Him as our Lord and Savior, we receive HIS LIFE— *God-life!* Christ's Spirit is imparted to us. We become one with Christ when His eternal Spirit lives in us.

That's what the Apostle Paul referred to when he wrote, *"I have been crucified with Christ and I no longer live, but* Christ lives in me. *The life I now live in the body, I live by faith in the Son of God, who loved me and gave himself for me"* (Galatians 2:20).

Upon receiving Christ, we who had no previous relationship with God because of sin, are not only officially and everlastingly *born into His family*, but *we are adopted* as well. (Ephesians 1:5) God, our Creator, becomes our Father. We become His children. The Holy Spirit becomes our *guide*. (John

16:13) Christ become our *elder brother*. Romans 8:29 refers to Him as the "first-born" among many brothers—us. Hebrews 2:11 tells us that He is not ashamed to call us His brothers.

So, everything not only began with a relationship between a Father and His Son, it will end with the Father and a house full of His children. In 2 Corinthians 6:18 we read, *"I will be a Father to you, and you will be My sons and daughters, says the Lord Almighty."* Jesus foretold this in John 14:2 when He said, *"My Father's house has many rooms; if that were not so, would I have told you that I am going there to prepare a place for you?"*

God is all about relationships. His first concern is that we establish our relationship with Him. Appendix A, in this book, explains how you can know Him. Because relationships are important to Him, His Word is filled with guidelines for various relationships:

- Parent and child
- Husband and wife
- Elder and younger
- Employer and employee
- And more.

Broken, God-approved relationships grieve Him.

Take marriage for example.

Too many people treat marriage casually. God hates divorce. (Malachi 2:16) God intends for marriage to be a visible image of Christ (the groom) and His Church (the bride), for whom He laid down His life.

Divorces damage lives, especially children. And in many cases where divorce has occurred, bitterness, anger and revenge are often the result. Later, we'll look at solutions for these. (Keep in mind, God loves and forgives divorced people.)

But first, let's consider relationships that *should be broken*. There are both God-approved and God-forbidden relationships.

Unequally Yoked

Scripture teaches that believers are not to be unequally yoked with nonbelievers. Because there can be no true fellowship between righteousness and unrighteousness. (2 Corinthians 6:14) In verses 16-18, Paul references passages in Leviticus 26:12; Ezekiel 37:27, and Isaiah 52:11.

Some, who were not aware of this command, or were and violated it by marrying a non-believer, wonder if they should divorce their unbelieving spouse. God's answer to that question is, "no." Why? For two reasons. First, as stated above, God hates divorce. The second reason is found in 1st Corinthians 7:12-16. Paul writes to the Church in Corinth:

> *To the rest* (To those living in 'mixed marriages,' believers with unbelievers,) *I say this (I, not the Lord): If any brother has a wife who is not a believer and she is willing to live with him, he must not divorce her.* [13] *And if a woman has a husband who is not a believer and he is willing to live with her, she must not divorce him.* (There is God's answer.) [14] *For the unbelieving husband has been sanctified through his wife, and the unbelieving wife has been sanctified through her believing husband. Otherwise your children would be unclean, but as it is, they are holy.*

What *does* this mean? It *does not* mean that the unbelieving spouse and children are saved. It's a mystery, for sure. It seems to suggest, among other possibilities, that the unbelieving spouse and/or child *benefit from their relationship* with the believing spouse. Perhaps it's in terms of God's blessing and protection.

The bottom line is that each person must experience Christ's salvation the same way—personally, and as Paul states in Ephesians 2:8-9, *"by grace, through faith."* NOTE: God has no in-laws or grandchildren, only sons and daughters. Then God says,

> *[15] But if the unbeliever leaves, let it be so. The* (saved) *brother or the sister <u>is not bound</u> in such circumstances;* (is unrestricted) *God has called us to live in peace. [16] How do you know, wife, whether you will save your husband? Or, how do you know, husband, whether you will save your wife?*

Verse 16 (above) offers an important clarification. Why? Because, sometimes the believing spouse feels forced to prevent the unbeliever from leaving, believing that they are the only key to the unbeliever's salvation. *They are not.* As believers, our only importance to the issue of another's salvation are our personal testimonies (integrity); and our witness. Beyond that, the unbeliever's relationship with God is a matter between Him and them. We aren't "co-saviors with Christ."

The only allowance for a believer to file for divorce, is found in Matthew 19:7-9. It is important to note that it's an allowance, not a command. Many refer to this allowance as the "exception clause."

Sadly, sometimes one's marriage partner rejects Christ and them, reconciliation is denied, and divorce is the only option.

Cruelty in Marriage

Some marriages involve cruelty, which can take many forms including emotional and physical cruelty. No one is to endanger themselves for the sake of a messed-up marriage. Ultimatums become necessary, like: "Either we get marital counseling, or I will move out." And, yes, separation (at least temporary) is sometimes called for. As one marriage counselor explained to an abused wife, "It sounds as if you need to move out temporarily and create a crisis for your abusive husband." Some people are only sensible in times of crisis.

[NOTE: No two people or marriages are the same. Every situation is different. Do not consider this as specific advice for you and your spouse. If you are in a dangerous marriage, contact a Christian marriage counselor immediately. Don't know where to find one? Call local churches and ask their pastoral staffs if they can recommend one.]

Unfortunately, when relationships go bad, emotions often run wild, and bad behavior follows. Out and out hatred can be born of a root of bitterness.

Please pray this with me: "Father, I want my relationships with others to demonstrate who You are. Teach me how to love the hard-to-love, as You do. Lord, I choose to follow you. In Jesus' Name I pray, amen."

Chapter 8

Hatred

As we all know, hate is an intense dislike for something or someone. However, there are many levels and expressions of hate. One might hate their employer; another might hate his job. One hates chocolate cake; another hates abortion.

The Surprising Reason We Hate

Hate is a natural human emotion. It's natural because God created us in His image. Though God is love, God also hates. How can that be? A mother who loves her child would hate illicit drugs to which her child is addicted. So, love and hate can coexist in the same heart.

- In Proverbs 8:13 we are told that to fear the Lord is to *hate evil.*
- Psalm 45:7 tells us to love righteousness and *hate wickedness.*
- Romans 12:9 instructs us to *hate evil* and love good.

In no case is the object of our hatred to be another person. God hates sin, but He loves sinners. Why is that?

Because, as said, God created man in His image. Satan created sin. Sin kills (Romans 6:23A). *"The soul that sinneth, it shall die"* (Ezekiel 18:20)

It is our sin that separates us from God. However, God loves us and sacrificed His Son, as payment for our sin.

Ephesians Chapter 4 offers us additional light on this issue, although at first it can be confusing. Confusing? Why?

Ephesians 4:26 seems to allow for anger in certain cases, but with a warning. He writes, *"Be angry and sin not."* Then in Ephesians 4:31, Paul instructs the Christians in Ephesus to *"put away all…anger."* So, which is it? Are we to be angry, or to put anger away?

The issue is resolved in the two meanings of the English word translated "anger" from the original language.

"Put away anger."

The anger we are to put away is *temper*. We believers are to be filled with the Spirit. (Ephesians 5:18) As Spirit-filled believers we will express the nine "fruit of the Spirit," Paul describes to us in Galatians 5:22. They are facets of the image of Christ, to whom we are to be being conformed. (Romans 8:29)

1. Love

2. Joy

3. Peace,

4. Long suffering (patience)

5. Gentleness

6. Goodness

7. Meekness

8. Self-control, and

9. Faith

We can easily see that outbursts of *temper* are violations of virtually all nine. So, a Spirit-filled believer will hold his temper. Anger? Yes. But, it's anger under control.

What about the anger *we are to experience,* yet sin not? (Vs 26)

Be angry.

There are times when believers encounter wickedness that angers them. "Abortion" immediately comes to mind. We certainly should be angry with the fact that more than one-half million babies are murdered in their mother's wombs each year. Eight five percent of those women are unmarried. If that doesn't anger us, something is seriously wrong.

However, we can be angry about that and not sin by exercising Spirit-empowered self-control, and releasing the issue to our Father, the righteous judge.

We are free to express our concern, but God warns us not to go to bed angry. One version says we are not to allow the sun to go down on our anger. Why? Paul says that for us to do so, is to *"give place to the devil."* It's to "leave an open door" to Satan.

Sadly, we most often see this with marital disputes. A husband and wife disagree, then argue, then they fail to reconcile and resolve the issue prior to retiring for the evening. By doing so, they leave a door open for the enemy. He does even more damage to their relationship.

You wouldn't think of retiring for the night with the doors of your home unlocked. Don't "spirit-doors" open to the devil and his demons. This explains how some divorces form so quickly.

Interestingly, these verses in Ephesians 4 are followed by what we were taught as children, "The Golden Rule."

"Be ye kind, one to the another, tender-hearted, forgiving one another."

What most of us were not taught about the *rule* is the degree to which we are to forgive.

The verse continues to tell how to forgive. Paul writes, *"Even as God for Christ's sake has forgiven us."*

How has the Father forgiven us? The Father, having accepted Christ's sacrificial death as payment in full for our sin against Him, releases us from all guilt, and promises never to bring them up again. *"For I will forgive their wickedness and will remember their sins no more"* (Hebrews 8:12).

What our omniscient God chooses to forget, He forgets completely!

Please pray this with me: "Father, teach me that I don't have to agree with someone to love them and fellowship with them. Forgive me for ever valuing my opinion above other people. You died for people, not for my opinion. I choose to love those with different opinions, for Christ's sake. In Jesus' Name I pray, amen."

Chapter 9

Navigating A Troubled Marriage

Someone has said that the key to never experiencing a divorce is to never marry. <smile>It is true that loving relationships require risk. Love is the glue that holds them together. As Paul wrote, *"And over all these virtues put on love, which binds them all together in perfect unity"* (Colossians 3:14).

In too many cases, people have committed to marriage before they have committed to, or even understood, love. What's one to do in that case? What do you do when you aren't in love with your spouse?

First, understand that although love can, and often does, produce feelings—although love is *not a feeling*. Love is an action. Said another way, love is not what we feel, it is what we do!

Jim and Ann had been married for several years. In time, they grew apart. One could say that they "fell out of love." Their affection for each other was gone. Each did their own thing. As far as *romance* was concerned, it was ancient history.

They had grown apart in other ways too. Ann seemed to be a scorekeeper. In fact, she kept a growing list, at least mentally, of Jim's offenses to which she could, and often did, refer. It seemed that when a disagreement reached particular pitch, she would pull it out and rehearse it again. How many times had she reminded him of things he'd said and done years ago? All it really did was exacerbate the matter at hand, irritate and sometimes infuriate Jim, and drive an additional wedge between them. He'd tune her out and, as they say, would allow it to go in one ear and out the other.

Jim, had by now, little attraction to Ann. She hardly seemed the girl he had fallen in love with years earlier. Ann too had little affection, if any, remaining.

They were advised to see a marriage counsellor. The counselor listened to their descriptions of how things were between them. Finally, she asked each if they were in love with the other. Both said, "no." Ann was already weeping. Jim simply wanted to leave.

The counselor then asked, when they had stopped loving each other. They both thought back through their feelings.

Before either could answer, she explained. "I'm not asking when you stopped *having loving feelings* for each other. I mean, when did you stop *doing loving things* for each other.

They could hardly relate to that question. "Why would I do loving things for someone we don't love," Jim wondered. Ann was also confused.

The wise counselor instantly recognized that when it came to a loving relationship, neither of them had a clue.

She said, "Let's look at what God says about this matter." She handed each of them this version of 1st Corinthians 13 — commonly referred to as *the love chapter*. Then she invited them to read it slowly, aloud with her, pausing to consider each phrase they read.

"If I speak in the tongues of men or of angels, but do not have love, I am only a resounding gong or a clanging cymbal.

² If I have the gift of prophecy and can fathom all mysteries and all knowledge, and if I have a faith that can move mountains, but do not have love I am nothing.

³ If I give all that I possesses to the poor and gives over my body to hardship that I may boast, but do not have love, I gain nothing.

⁴ I am patient, I am kind. I do not envy, I do not boast, I am not proud.

⁵ I do not dishonor others,

I am not self-seeking,

I am not easily angered,

I keep no record of wrongs.

⁶ I do not delight in evil but rejoice with the truth.

⁷ I always protect, always trust, always hope, and always persevere.

⁸ Love never fails. But where there are prophecies, they will cease; where there are tongues, they will be

stilled; where there is knowledge, it will pass away. 9 For we know in part and we prophesy in part, 10 but when completeness comes, what is in part disappears.

11 When I was a child, I talked like a child, I thought like a child, I reasoned like a child. When I became an adult, I left the ways of childhood behind.

12 For now we see only a reflection as in a mirror; then we shall see face to face. Now I know in part; then I shall know fully, even as I am fully known.

13 And now these three remain: faith, hope and love. But the greatest of these is love."

The counselor continued, "You two stopped loving (doing loving things for) each other some time ago. You stopped because the feelings of love were no longer there. What you must do is reverse the process.

Don't do loving things because of how you feel. We feel what we feel as a result of what we do. Acts of love produce and nourish loving feelings.

Ann, at some point, you began keeping a list of everything you felt Jim did wrong. Doing that began to change your heart toward him. By expressing it to him, it began to change his heart toward you. The wife who at one time had shown him honor and respect, was now behaving as his judge. What normal man could nurture genuine loving feelings toward his judge?

Jim, you once adored Ann. She was your princess. But as time passed, you became sloppy in doing loving things for her. You put business and pleasure ahead of her. You stayed late at the office, where you were boss and were held in high esteem.

A man's greatest need, Ann, is to be honored, to feel respected. Jim, a woman's greatest need is to be treasured. You are the one to whom God has assigned that primary responsibility. You two can and should rekindle the fire that has gone out. The embers are still there. They must be fueled and fanned into a flame.

Here is what I want you to do.

1. Make a list of 10 things you like about each other. No matter how small or insignificant they may seem.
2. Every day, do three things with one of those 10;
    a. Thank God for it.
    b. Mention it to someone else in conversation.

    c. Thank each other for that quality.

Ann, tear up your list, and release Jim as God has released you from your sins, never to remember them against you again. Never remind Jim of them again.

Jim, begin to do the things you once did. Bring home flowers or chocolates. Take Ann for a date at least twice a month. Compliment her often for things she does, and more importantly, for who she is. Open doors for her.

Each of you consider a task around the house that the other hates to do and make it *your* new assignment—in service to the each other.

Hold hands.

Greet and leave each other with a kiss.

The nursery rhyme says that after his great fall, 'No one could put Humpty Dumpty together again.' But you two can renew your marriage, your love; and your best days can be before you.

In a very short time, you'll find those feelings of love following those loving actions."

Jim and Ann admitted that as they left the counselor's office, neither of them had much confidence in their new assignments. But then, nothing else had seemed to work for them.

Jim opened the door as they left. Ann took Jim's hand as they walked through the parking lot to their car.

This time, Jim didn't automatically turn on the radio, they actually talked to each other on the way home.

Day-by-day they each worked, at first, without feelings. But as they did, they discovered it was true. Feelings *do* follow actions, and not the other way around. Their feelings of love were being fueled by the loving things they did. The tensions they had previously lived with rarely appeared. When they did, they caught themselves, and didn't allow it to fester into an argument.

That was many years ago. Today, they continue to enjoy each other. Ann is Jim's greatest cheerleader, and Jim adores his bride.

NOTE: To respect and esteem each other better than oneself is the nature of the kingdom! (Philippians 2:3)

Please pray this with me: "Lord, help me apply these principles and truths in my own relationships with others. I choose to refuse to hold grudges and to tear up lists, even mental lists, of wrongs. I realize that just as Your Son's death paid my sin debt in full, He was dying for the sins of the world. So, whether they do or not, I accept Jesus' love-payment for them, and release them. In Jesus' Name I pray, amen."

Let go of grudges.
You don't hold a grudge. A grudge holds you.

Chapter 10

The Ministry of Reconciliation

As we've seen, all of creation began with our eternal God, His Spirit, and His Son—the eternal Three-in-One—a relationship. Though He is a relational being within Himself, He longed for additional meaningful relationships. The fact that He has chosen you and me with whom to relate is beyond comprehension. Yet, ours isn't to understand why—it's to gratefully and humbly accept His gracious invitation to an eternal relationship with Him through His Son, Jesus.

Notice these *plural* references that our ONE true God uses for Himself. John wrote, *"In the beginning was the Word* (Jesus), *and the Word (Jesus) <u>was with</u> God, and the Word (Jesus) <u>was</u> God. ² He (Jesus) <u>was with God</u> in the beginning. ³ Through him (Jesus) all things were made"* (John 1:1-3a) To be *with someone*, requires that there be at least two, doesn't it? Yet the two, along with the Holy Spirit, were also one. Sure enough, in Genesis 1:26a we read, *"Then God said, "<u>Let us</u> make mankind in our image, in <u>our likeness</u>. . ."*

Throughout this book, I've reminded you how each of our lives involves an assortment of relationships. To manage them properly, is not only one of our primary responsibilities, it is central to our success in living to glorify God and reach our kingdom potential. Thankfully God's Word provides us with guidelines for virtually every relationship we have, which means that God is not only concerned about them but has expectations for us concerning them.

Here are a few:

- True friendship (Proverbs 17:17; John 15:13; Ephesians 4:2-3)
- Employers (Colossians 3:23)
- Marriage (Proverbs 31:10-11; Genesis 2:18; Genesis 2:24)
- Parents (Exodus 20:12; Ephesians 6:1-3)

- Children (Psalm 127:3)
- Others (Hebrews 10:24-25; 1 Peter 4:10; Hebrews 10:24)
- God (Psalm 37:3-4; 1 Peter 5:6-7; 2 Corinthians 5:17-18)
- Dating (1 Corinthians 6:18; 1 Corinthians 15:33; 2 Corinthians 6:14)
- There are many, many others.

One thing to keep in mind is that successful relationships in any area of our lives will require God's presence.

So, whether it's your job or your marriage, the place and the priority you give God in it, will determine your success.

The bottom line is that the Bible is a guidebook for relationships *with God* and others. In John 15, Jesus describes us as branches that will only find our significance by remaining attached to the Vine—Christ. Similarly, Paul teaches us in 1 Corinthians 14 that we are members of the same Body—the Body of Christ. As believers, we find our individual value as members of the Body, attached to the Vine--in relationship with others.

Unity doesn't mean uniformity. The God of unity is also God of diversity. He has given us different personalities, spiritual gifts and kingdom assignments. No one has your fingerprints or DNA, for example. It's a matter of blending our differences into meaningful God-honoring relationships that represent Him here and extend His kingdom throughout the Earth.

In this book I've sought to offer counsel on how to maintain healthy relationships with others, and to show how our relationship with God depends on how we treat others.

Because relationships are central to His plan for us, our relationships will be continually tested. Why? God allows us to be tested, as He did with Job, to teach us and to give us opportunities to demonstrate our obedience and commitment to Him and to each other.

In closing, I'd like to remind you of a profound truth, we learned earlier. According to Jesus, we are to forgive those who've offended us seventy times seven—or endlessly, as He forgives us. And as we've learned, for us to do so doesn't mean to overlook or minimize the offence. His disciples rightly pointed out that that would require a significant measure of faith. Faith based on what?

We base our forgiveness on His payment, not theirs. It does no good to wait for and hope for the one(s) who've offended us to repent and apologize. We are to forgive them quickly and completely based on two things.

1. Based on the way He's forgiven us.
2. Based on the price He has already paid, and the punishment He has already received for their sin.

Of course, there is no way to cover everything with respect to relationships. To this point, I've tried to share some biblical life-principles I've learned and by which I attempt to live.

I don't know how you feel when you discover a new biblical perspective about life, but to me it's like when I was a child on Christmas morning. I can hardly wait to unwrap and open it to see what more is inside. And perhaps like you, the deeper I look, the more exciting things I discover. Spiritual truth is amazing like that.

Our eternal self-revealing God and Father meets our needs moment-by-moment, layer-by-layer, truth-by-truth yet always leaves us hungering for more. What an amazing Lord! The song is right. "He's a good, good Father. That's who He is."

So, we release our offenders and in so doing, we ourselves go free! Jesus not only died for you. He died for your enemies. As you trusted Him and His payment for *your sin*, for your forgiveness; you are to trust His payment for theirs and release them with your blessings. *That* is the power of the gospel!

A profound example

Jesus, who challenged us to love our enemies, demonstrated this teaching in such an amazingly clear way the night before He was betrayed.

At what we frequently refer to as "the last supper" in John 13:21-30 Jesus predicted His betrayal when He said,

> *"'Very truly I tell you, one of you is going to betray me.'*
>
> *[22] His disciples stared at one another, at a loss to know which of them he meant.[23] One of them, the disciple whom Jesus loved, was reclining next to him. [24] Simon Peter motioned to this disciple and said, 'Ask him which one he means.'*
>
> *[25] Leaning back against Jesus, he asked him, 'Lord, who is it?'*
>
> *[26] Jesus answered, 'It is the one to whom I will give this piece of bread when I have dipped it in the dish.' Then, dipping the piece of bread, he gave it to Judas, the son*

of Simon Iscariot. ²⁷ As soon as Judas took the bread, Satan entered into him.

So Jesus told him, 'What you are about to do, do quickly.' ²⁸ But no one at the meal understood why Jesus said this to him. ²⁹ Since Judas had charge of the money, some thought Jesus was telling him to buy what was needed for the festival, or to give something to the poor. ³⁰ As soon as Judas had taken the bread, he went out."

The question is, "What did Jesus do, knowing in advance that in a matter of hours, Judas would betray Him to be crucified for 30 pieces of silver?"

1. Jesus fed Judas, along with His other disciples.
2. Jesus washed Judas' feet, along with washing His other disciple's feet.
3. Jesus didn't return evil for evil. He loved Judas, the one He knew would betray Him.

In fact, Jesus would have even died for Judas's sins. Sadly, Judas went out and hanged himself before Jesus was crucified. He missed the Christ's resurrection.

It shouldn't surprise us to read this in Romans 5:8-10,

"But God demonstrates his own love for us in this: While we were still sinners, Christ died for us. ⁹ Since

> *we have now been justified by his blood, how much more shall we be saved from God's wrath through him!* ¹⁰ *For if, while we were God's enemies, we were reconciled to him through the death of his Son, how much more, having been reconciled, shall we be saved through his life!"*

Again, in 2 Corinthians 5:11-21, we read, "...*God, who reconciled us to himself through Christ and <u>gave us the ministry of reconciliation</u>.*"

What do we do, if after forgiving one who has sinned against us, for one reason or another, we are unable to reconcile and establish peace between us and them?

That will sometimes be the case. Paul resolves that dilemma for us in Romans 12:18, after teaching us how to forgive, and how to treat those who have offended us by not repaying evil with evil, he writes, *"If it is possible on your part, live at peace with everyone."* While we *can* be reconciled with anyone in our own hearts, there will be some who will not reciprocate. Our obligation before God is *to do what is possible* on our part. God bless you and your ministry of reconciliation.

Regarding betrayal. Joseph was innocent, yet imprisoned. However, he wasn't in prison. He was in a process. What did he do to deal with his betrayal? He focused on God's purpose, rather than his pain. God was preparing him for his destiny. Had he focused on his circumstances he'd never have discovered it. He focused on his gifts and assignments. That is how he discovered his destiny.

Now know that I am praying for you, and everyone who reads this book.

APPENDIX A:
How to Be Born Again

In December 1967, the world heard a startling announcement. South African surgeon (and preacher's son) Dr. Christiaan Barnard had performed the world's first human heart transplant. He'd placed the heart of Denise Darvall, a woman in her mid-twenties who died in an automobile accident, inside the chest of fifty-five-year-old diabetic Louis Washkansky, who had incurable heart disease. The new heart was actually beating on its own! That, my friend, although fairly common today, was amazing.

When the interviewer asked Dr. Barnard why he had decided to perform such a risky operation, his answer caught my attention: "One look at Mr. Washkansky, and I knew he couldn't live with that old heart." I will never forget the day that I realized that I too couldn't live with my old heart. If you've never had one, you also need a heart transplant, not a physical heart transplant, but a spiritual one.

God's Word tells us, *"The heart is deceitful above all things, and desperately wicked"* (Jeremiah 17:9). It says that *"all (of us) have sinned and come short of the glory of God"* (Romans 3:23). We all have a "spiritual heart disease" that is always fatal, for *"the wages of sin is death"* (Romans 6:23). This spiritual death is separation from God, in this life and for eternity. We're beyond the need of a spiritual heart massage-only a new heart will do. Everyone needs a new heart.

Good news! God loves you. He wants you to experience peace and eternal, abundant life. Today He says to you, *"A new heart also will I give you . . . and I will take away the stony heart out of your flesh"* (Ezekiel 36:26). The heavenly Father wants to perform the transplant you need. You cannot pay for the operation because Jesus Christ already paid the price when He died for your sins and mine on the cross. Today you can have a new, clean, pure heart by doing just as David the psalmist did. He asked God for it: *"Create in me a clean heart, 0 God"* (Psalm 51: 10). And guess what--the Lord did!

God didn't create us to be like robots who'd automatically obey and serve Him. He created us in his image and gave us freedom to choose for or against Him.

Like the first man and woman, Adam and Eve, who chose their own way in the Garden of Eden and sinned against God, we too have chosen to disobey Him and go our own way. The result is that our sin has separated us from God.

Worse still, as hard as we may try, and regardless of our good intentions, there is no way we can be reconciled to God apart from

Jesus Christ. Only Christ and His cross can reconnect us to God.

Jesus died on the cross and rose from the grave to pay the penalty for our sin and bridge the gap between God and us.

Here is the solution:

(1) Admit that you've sinned against God.

(2) Acknowledge that you need a Savior, that you cannot save yourself.

(3) Repent by turning from your sins.

(4) Believe in your heart that Jesus died for you and that the Father raised Him from the dead on the third day. He is alive!

(5) Now trust Jesus Christ as your personal Lord and Savior by inviting Him to live in your heart through His Holy Spirit.

Are you ready? Good!

Right now, right where you are, turn to God and say,

> *Dear God,*
>
> *I have sinned against you. I am a sinner. I need your forgiveness. I need a new, clean heart. Today, I turn from my sins. Forgive and cleanse me. I trust you as my Savior and give my life to you. Come into my heart today, Risen Christ, and be Lord of my life. I choose to follow you. Thank you for the new life you've given me.*

Thank you for my new, clean heart. In Jesus' name, I pray. Amen.

Did you sincerely turn to Christ? Did you invite Him into your life? Then congratulations! He has washed away your sins and now lives in you. This is what the Scripture calls being born again, a supernatural work of God's Spirit, who is now in your heart.

www.ingramcontent.com/pod-product-compliance
Lightning Source LLC
Chambersburg PA
CBHW052108070526
44584CB00017B/2392